Contents

<u>About The Author</u>

Last Call:

Understanding and Treating the Alcoholic Brain

By C.K. Murray

Join the Newsletter

Similar works by C.K. Murray:

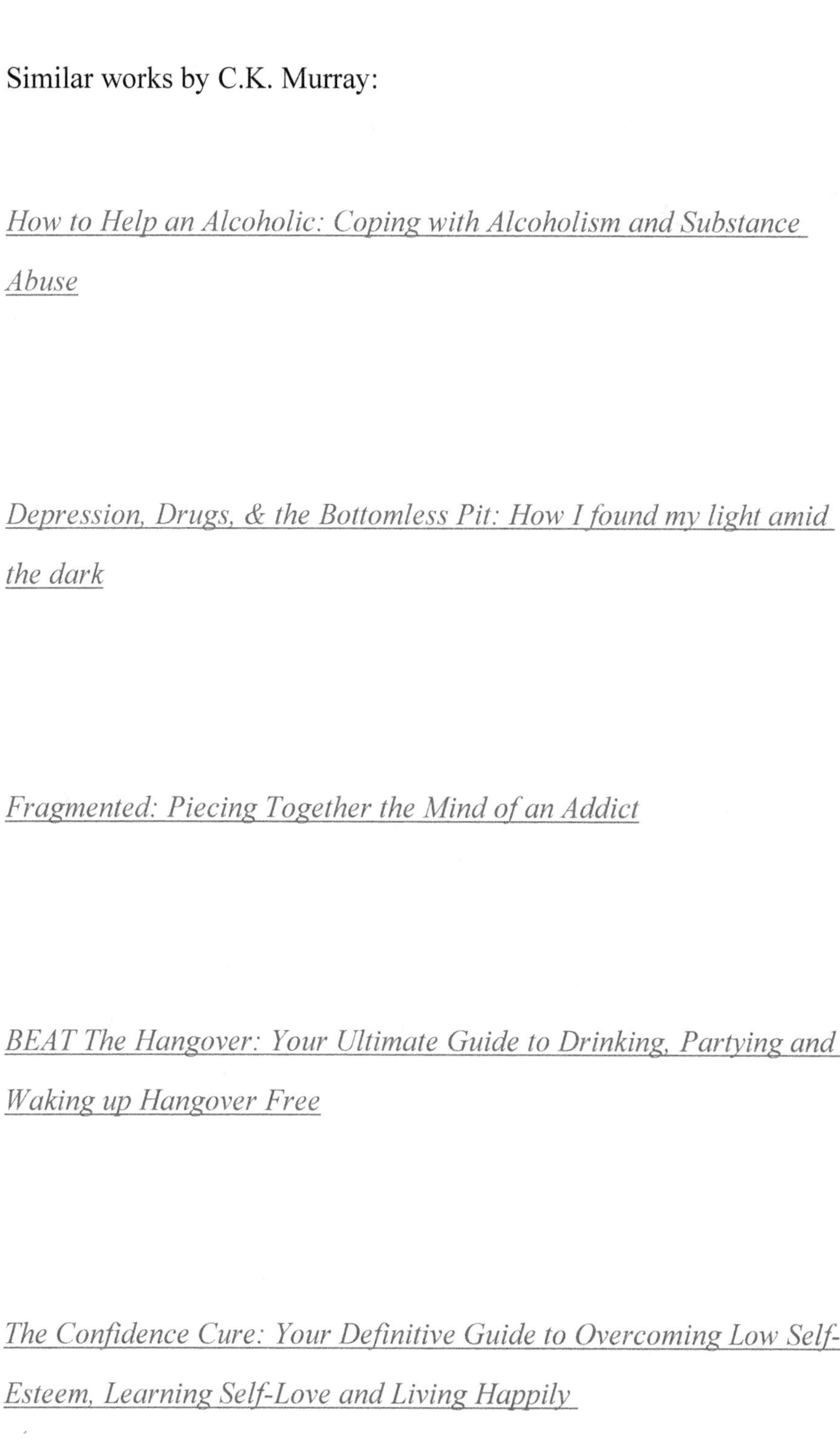

How to Help an Alcoholic: Coping with Alcoholism and Substance Abuse

Depression, Drugs, & the Bottomless Pit: How I found my light amid the dark

Fragmented: Piecing Together the Mind of an Addict

BEAT The Hangover: Your Ultimate Guide to Drinking, Partying and Waking up Hangover Free

The Confidence Cure: Your Definitive Guide to Overcoming Low Self-Esteem, Learning Self-Love and Living Happily

Dear Friend or Family Member:

Let's be honest. You probably don't know where to begin. Sure, you *want* to help that person you love or care for, but how? There's a lot of *stuff* out there, and it all claims a different problem and a different remedy. Chances are, all this talk of abuse, addiction and alcoholism keeps your head spinning.

What does any of it mean?

As the friend or family member of a person addicted to alcohol, you oftentimes find yourself scratching your head. Why can't they just put the drink down? Can't they see that it's ruining them? Don't they realize how alcohol has negatively affected their life and the lives of those who love them? Why are they being so selfish?

Just put the drink down!

Except, it's not nearly so easy. It's easy to think, sure. It's easy to think how most people think, because, well, *most* people don't think the way an alcoholic thinks.

Still, like anybody, alcoholics have their shapes and sizes. They have their colors and their places. They come from every conceivable background and belief system, and most of the time they're right in front of our faces—if we even notice.

Alcoholics can be deceptive. They can be lovable and loving, even seeming at times to be the warmest people in our lives. And maybe they are. The problem is, they don't think this.

Again, for the alcoholic, it is their thinking that is their problem. Their enemy; their destruction.

"Alcohol isn't my problem," they might tell you. "It's the symptom."

Many people have ways of dealing with life, but alcoholics decided on theirs a long time ago, and they are *damn* set on keeping it.

Many alcoholics never admit what they deep down know to be true. Or they'll joke about it. They'll employ a variety of defense mechanisms to deny or minimize their addiction to alcohol. Hell, at times their alcohol use may actually seem to *improve* their lives.

And then the darkness rears its lovely head.

This is when things can go bad, real bad. But things don't always have to go real bad. Not every alcoholic will be blatantly abusive or self-destructive. For some drinkers, alcoholism is an extremely slow, and long, and degenerative monster. It will erode their abilities, weaken their relationships and tarnish their character.

Some alcoholics define themselves differently. They might call themselves "addicts." To these individuals, alcohol is merely the vice of choice. The marker of a greater issue.

They will tell you that if they weren't drinking, they would be doing something else to an extreme. It may be no surprise then, that many recovering alcoholics abuse caffeine and cigarettes.

Again, alcohol is the symptom, not the source, of the problem.

So then what is the problem? Why can't alcoholics just get it together like other people—why are they so dependent on a fluid? Can't they just learn to be stronger?

We are often surprised by people who drink. *I never knew it was that bad*, we might think. *I just don't get it, she has everything going for her.*

People who drink use alcohol to numb their problems. Just become a person appears to have a great life filled with great *things*, that doesn't mean we know what goes on inside them. We can't always determine the thoughts and emotions a person experiences. There is always more than meets the eye.

When you think of alcohol, think of coffee. Just as many people may wake in the morning to drink some coffee, alcoholics may rise to the burn of a stiff drink. Like coffee-drinkers, alcoholics are in a routine. Coffee drinkers want that fresh brew in the morning. It gets them going, it's part of their day—heck, they might drink two or three or four cups of coffee *throughout* the day. Alcoholics are not much different. If they go too long without their alcohol, they notice a difference. They don't like that difference because it is uncomfortable; unfamiliar. Think about it. When people don't have coffee, they get tired and they get headaches, and they generally don't feel 'right.'

I need my coffee, we might joke. *Don't talk to me till I've had my coffee.* Although there are plenty of differences between regular coffee-drinkers and alcoholics, there are fundamental similarities as well. Both hate going without their fix. They hate the difference between how they feel and how they want to feel. Whether caffeine or alcohol, the effect is real. For alcoholics, not having alcohol makes things feel out-of-whack, and when things are out-of-whack, the alcoholic begins to think about everything *else* that can go 'out-of-whack.'

Alcohol is a source of strength. Or so the alcoholic believes. The problem is, it's a false strength; a shield. A suit of armor that slowly wears the body and deadens the mind.

When we take that armor off, we feel worn and tired. But we also feel naked. And for the alcoholic, feeling naked—feeling exposed—is simply too much. Showing one's true colors, one's sober shades, is unbearable.

Alcoholism is a disease of the mind, it is a real disease that changes the chemical levels and connections of our brain. When alcoholics drink, they suddenly feel better. The feeling is temporary, but the alcoholic does not care. As long as the alcohol is in their blood, they will be fine.

Whatever is coming, whatever stressor the future brings, the alcoholic will be ready. His weapon against living is drawn. Her bottle is never empty.

Dear Drinker:

If you're reading this, you've come to a decision. You've decided that you're tired. You're tired of living day after day, night into night, doing the same thing. You're angry, you're lost, you're hopeless and hurting.

You *need* to stop drinking but you don't know how.

Maybe you don't know if you're strong enough. Perhaps you think it's impossible. Maybe you've tried and failed, and tried and failed, and after so many tries, you've given up. Maybe you finally stopped caring…

If this sounds like you, you are not alone. In fact, there are millions upon millions of others *just* like you, struggling to cope, and struggling to get through their day to day worries without the bottle.

Maybe you like wine. Perhaps you're a liquor type, throwing back anything you can get your hands on. Or maybe you have a refined palette, settling only for the finest—constantly flooding your body and brain with the best sauce success can buy. Perhaps you don't care what *it* is, as long as *it* is inside you.

Whether wine-drinker, or cheap boozer, or liqueur connoisseur, you've got a problem. It's taken you a lot of time and thought and painful self-reflection, but if you're reading this, you've *got* to be honest.

You have a problem. You have an addiction. You have a disease of the mind.

This problem has affected many areas of your life, if not all of them. For the longest time you thought you were fine. Even as others told you otherwise, you continued on, blindly. You denied and you joked and you laughed and you did everything you could to hide the truth. You pulled your thoughts and feelings away from the world because it was too much—because *you* were right, and *they* were wrong.

Because nobody, *nobody*, could tell you how to live your life.

But now that life is slipping. And what are the reasons? Is it family? Did somebody you trust or love finally lay into you? Did you lose somebody? Was it a break-up, a separation, a divorce—a death?

Are you struggling with everyday things? Are you in financial trouble? Do you find that the only way to stop thinking about all the bullshit is to numb it all away? Is that it? Or how about the law? Did you get a DUI? Were you drunk in public? Have you been before lawyers, and judges, and bailiffs, and jail guards? Have you tried the AA meetings, that 12-step *thing*, the whole group therapy this, and individual therapy that, feeling—once upon a time—that maybe you had it, *maybe* you were making progress… only to fall off?

What's the source of your pain? Your fear? Your self-hate? What is keeping you from facing the world with a sober mind? Do you even know? Can you even remember? Or is it all too much? So overwhelming and confusing that you don't know when it started, when it all went south?

The most important thing you need to know *right now* is that you have the strength to change. Nobody else is going to change your ways. Your wife can leave you, you can lose your job, your friends, your bank account and your meaning—but if *you* don't act, none of this will matter. You may relapse again and again, but in the end, the choice is yours. You can pull yourself up, time and time again, moving closer, learning, striving, and enduring the oftentimes harrowing process of recovery. Or you can let it all slip.

Self-love is something we must learn. Experiences, genetic differences, and environmental factors can all affect this, but it's ultimately up to us. We are the ones in control. And as much as we don't believe it, as much as we have failed—we can now succeed.

Our journey starts today…

Alcoholic

It's a word we're all familiar with. We hear it on the news, in the movies, in jokes and conversations. It's a stigma, it's an irony; it's a disease that many people deny exists.

Drunk

To many of us, when we think of alcoholics, we think of *drunks*. These are the people we've all seen or imagined, swaying with bottle in hand, their faces flushed and their words slurred, and their glassy eyes half-crooked as they make their way.

But what about the successful business owner? What about the woman with the high-powered career? The same lady who returns home every day, after a long day, to flood her void with pricey wine? What about the man whose business is slipping out from under him, the man who keeps his booze close at bay, hidden away in the third drawer of his office desk?

There's always more than meets the eye, and some people either forget this or deny it altogether. Alcoholism doesn't have to be obvious. It doesn't have to turn a person into a vomiting, stumbling sloth.

Sometimes, the more subtle the addiction, the more destructive it is. Those who hide it the most may feel it the worst.

And we may never notice.

As a recovering alcoholic and drug addict, my experiences have taken me from the darkest voids in the deepest pits, to the highest of highs. Moments of invulnerability have been faced by epiphanies of deathly fragility.

The inner workings of the alcoholic's mind still leave researchers largely puzzled. Although the pieces are coming together, the theories continue to change, and the complexities continue to show. Nonetheless, we *are* making strides.

If you are an alcoholic, you are *not* alone.

A Starting Point

In the 5th edition of the <u>Diagnostic and Statistical Manual of Mental Disorders (DSM V)</u>, the category for addictive behavior is now *Substance-related and Addictive Disorders*. One of the main criteria for an addictive disorder is a craving or "strong desire" to use a substance.

But what constitutes "strong"? And even more, what's wrong with having a "desire"? Don't we all desire things from time to time? Even if that desire has great intensity, even if it is "strong," is that really such a bad thing? Or am I simply arguing semantics?

Given the psychiatric and societal impacts of the DSM, these categorizations are always changing. Certain criteria for one disorder will be removed, replaced, tweaked, expounded, and/or condensed—all in accordance with evolving clinical practice.

The truth is: alcoholism is real. It just isn't easily diagnosed.

Let me say that again. Alcoholism is *real*. It's as real as ADHD,

OCD, anxiety, depression, heart disease—you name it. It's a disorder, it's a disease. It's a progressive, chronic illness that can end in death.

Research shows that alcoholism is not only costly on the personal level, but is also a killing blow to our global society. According to the World Health Organization (WHO), the harmful use of alcohol results in approximately 2.5 million deaths each year. It is a major global contributing factor to death, disease and injury, ranging from everything to dependence, liver cirrhosis, cancers, and injuries, and including dangerous actions like drunk driving and violent incidents.

In fact, the WHO has listed alcohol as a causal factor in 60 different diseases and injuries and a component factor in 200 others. Roughly 4% of all deaths worldwide are directly correlated with alcohol, greater than the totals attributed HIV/AIDS, violence or tuberculosis. 320,000 people between the age of 15 and 29 die each year due to alcohol-related causes, comprising 9% of all deaths in the age group.

Alcohol is especially dangerous to men, given the male tendency to abuse alcohol. It is the number one risk factor for deaths in males aged 15–59, mainly due to injuries, violence and cardiovascular issues. Globally, 6.2% of all male deaths are attributed to alcohol with only a little over 1% of female deaths attributed to the substance.

Bottom line: Alcohol is lethal.

And easy to get. For addicts, the prevalence of alcohol in most societies only compounds the addictive drive. When we drive down the road, we see stores with the words "liquor" and "beer." We watch alcohol commercials on T.V., we see billboards and beer trucks, it's in movies and television shows, explicitly and implicitly present in almost every walk of life. Alcohol is in your restaurants, it's at our sporting events, it is even considered the cornerstone of many special occasions and holidays. And if you happen to go to a typical college, well, you *better* believe alcohol is going to be a major presence. Greek life and alcohol practically go hand-in-hand.

The truth is clear, alcohol is everywhere. It is so firmly engrained in our culture, that to avoid it would be nearly impossible. You would practically have to lock yourself in a sensory deprivation tank. And even then, there's no telling what alcohol-related thoughts your brain might conjure.

As a result of the inculcation of alcohol in most societies, it's no wonder that people become alcoholics.

Still, what is an "alcoholic"?

Many people enjoy moderate drinking, defined as 1 drink per day for women or 2 for men—is that bad?

In fact, for younger people, many attitudes and behaviors that are considered normal are then later in life frowned upon. We've all heard of binge-drinking and heavy drinking. Research shows that people below the age of 20 usually drink about 5 drinks at one time.

Is that bad?

Sometimes, it's easy to know when we've gone too far. People will vomit, they'll 'black out,' they'll make rash and foolish decisions that end poorly. In some cases, it even ends in alcohol poisoning. Symptoms of this bodily shut-down include confusion; difficulty remaining conscious; vomiting; seizures; breathing problems; low heart rate; clammy skin; dull responses, and exceedingly low body temperature.

But still… aren't these just cases of excessive drinking?

What's the difference between somebody who likes to drink excessively from time to time, and somebody who is an "alcoholic"?

The question is a good one, and the answer is hard to find. This is because most people are either unwilling to admit a problem, or honestly don't know what the heck makes it "a problem."

It can be easy to argue semantics. If we don't want a word or term to apply to us, it won't. If we feel that we're not drinking "excessively," that alcohol is not impacting "daily functioning," that we don't spend "a lot of time" drinking or acquiring or thinking about drinking, then we won't work to fix the "problem."

Having a problem with alcohol will obviously vary from person to person, context to context, culture to culture, etc. It will depend on a variety of factors and may often be referred to in other terms besides "alcoholism." People might talk of "abuse" and "dependence" and "use" and "addiction."

Although the terms themselves are not as important as improving the life circumstances of a struggling individual, having a grip on the 'lingo' can at least advance the discourse. That is to say, by having formal terms to describe the complex psychological and physical disease of alcoholism, we begin to make headway. We begin to talk about it.

And talking about the nefarious nature of disease, of alcoholism, is the first step in recognizing how it has impacted our lives.

The Lingo

So what are the terms and what do they mean? Where do we get the words we hear? The ones echoed by so-called experts, on television, in mental health manuals, guidelines, and diagnostic tools—who decided to use them and how are they used?

As you know, every society has a different method to their madness. Diagnoses are influenced as much by the study of addiction as they are by the social and political climate. Alcohol has been shown to be a major moneymaker, a staple of many cultural events, and so is definitely here to stay. Some countries are more liberal, others crack down as much as they can. Depending upon the nation, the state, the province, county, or jurisdiction—alcohol takes on a different attitude with a different behavior.

In order to account for these countless cultural deviations, the World Health Organization (WHO) has forged a clear list of words that pertain to alcohol and alcohol abuse. Take a look, familiarize yourself, and arm yourself with the words. Whether you're an alcoholic, just a 'normal' drinker, or somebody who knows an alcoholic, these terms can help:

Addiction: Repetitive use of a psychoactive substance or substances, so that the individual is periodically or chronically intoxicated, is compelled to take the preferred substance (or substances), is mostly incapable of voluntarily ceasing or modifying substance use behaviors, and is determined to obtain psychoactive substances by virtually any means.

It is regarded by many as a discrete disease affliction, a progressive disorder rooted in the pharmacological effects of the drug, and in the unique brain chemistry the alcoholic brings to the table. Addiction is usually not a diagnostic term, but is very widely used by professionals and the general public alike. Typically, addiction includes tolerance and withdrawal syndrome.

Alcoholism: A term of long-standing use and variable meaning, used to refer to chronic continual drinking or periodic consumption of alcohol which is marked by diminished control over drinking, frequent periods of intoxication, and preoccupation with alcohol and alcohol consumption despite negative consequences.

The term alcoholism was originally coined in 1849 by Magnus Huss. In the 1940s it referred to the physical consequences of chronic heavy drinking A narrower conceptualization of alcoholism is that it is a disease characterized by loss of control over drinking, brought on by a pre-existing biological anomaly, and having a predictable progressive trajectory.

The inexactness of the term caused a 1979 WHO Expert Committee to formulate alcohol dependence syndrome as one among a wide range of alcohol-related problems. Other formulations have split alcoholism into different types, some regarded as diseases and some not. Distinctions are made between essential alcoholism and reactive alcoholism, where "essential" indicates that alcoholism is not secondary to or brought on by some other condition.

Dependence: As applied to alcohol, the term implies a need for repeated doses of the substance to feel good or to avoid feeling bad. Dependence refers to both physical and psychological elements. Psychological or psychic dependence refers to the experience of impaired control over drinking or drug use, while physiological or physical dependence refers to tolerance and withdrawal symptoms.

Detoxification: The process by which an individual withdraws from the effects of a psychoactive substance. In clinical procedures, it is the withdrawal process conducted in a safe and effective manner, so that withdrawal symptoms are diminished. The facility in which this takes place may be termed a detoxification center, detox center, or sobering-up station.

Detoxification may or may not involve the administration of medications. When it does, the medication dose is calculated to relieve the withdrawal syndrome without inducing intoxication, and is gradually tapered off while the patient recovers. The term "self-detoxification" is used to denote unassisted recovery from intoxication or withdrawal symptoms.

Tolerance: A diminished response to a drug dose that occurs with continuing use. Increased doses of alcohol or other drugs are required to get the effects originally brought on by lower doses. Tolerance can occur as functional tolerance, a decrease in sensitivity of the central nervous system to the substance; behavioral tolerance, a change in the effect of a drug as a result of learning environmental change; and acute tolerance, a rapid, transient acclimation to the effect of a substance after a single dose. There is also the concept of reverse tolerance, aka sensitization, which refers to increased responses to a substance with repeated use.

Withdrawal syndrome: A cluster of symptoms of varying severity which occur on cessation or reduction of use of a psychoactive substance that has been used repetitively, usually for a long period and/ or in large doses. The syndrome is characterized by signs of physiological disturbance.

The alcohol withdrawal syndrome is marked by tremor, sweating, anxiety, agitation, depression, nausea, and malaise. It happens 6-48 hours after cessation of alcohol consumption and, when unimpeded, lessens after 2-5 days. It may be complicated by grand mal seizures and may progress to delirium (known as delirium tremens).

Alrighty then, so now you know. Right?

Or maybe not. Perhaps, you're so confused you feel that having read those terms only made things worse. If you're anything like me, you've got your issues. You might take offense with certain words, or find other definitions dubious or strange or inapplicable. All in all, maybe you feel like it's all a load of horseshit.

If so, I don't blame you. Even though I've been sober for years now, that doesn't mean I necessarily buy everything that is fed to me. I still have my doubts, and there are definitely operational definitions that still make me simmer.

The thing you need to remember is, if you have a problem with alcohol, only you can admit it. If your friend or family member has a problem with alcohol, only they can admit it. All the jail time, family trouble, financial struggle, hate, pain, and indiscretion in the world won't make an alcoholic address a problem unless that individual is ready to change. Truth to oneself is the name of the game. Honesty, honesty, honesty.

The problem is, we're all capable of bullshit. We like to make up stuff and pretend stuff and self-delude till the moon comes apart. It is part of human nature. Sometimes, the truth is too hard to face, so we ignore it. We numb it. We find ways to keep it hidden away, locked away, gone and forgotten.

If you or somebody you care for is struggling with alcohol, it is time to be honest. Better yet, it's time to understand *why*.

It's time to understand why we act the way we do. Why we *just* can't admit the problem, the way we should.

Defense Mechanisms

As previously stated, the only way to address the problems caused by alcohol is to admit that alcohol is a problem. Simple enough, right?

Uh… wrong.

It's actually really hard, and for us alcoholics, it's also really easy. It's easy to bullshit ourselves and others because we've been doing it for so long; it's engrained. Like any habit, we know how and when to do it, the way we have always done it. And when lying to ourselves and others becomes a problem, when we start to feel bad about the whole thing—then what do we do?

Well, we drink.

But let's not drink. Let's take some time to face our fears. Honesty hurts, but pumping your brain and heart and every inch of your circulatory system with the alcohol toxin is even worse. *Honestly.*

So stop hurting and start healing. Take the first step toward recovery, and look at the way you think. Understand why you deny what is clearly a problem in the eyes of those who know you. Examine the way you think. This is important—the way we think is often the way we behave.

In thinking of how we think and how we avoid our issues, we can look no further than Freud. That's right, Sigmund Freud, the dude who is well known for dreams and icebergs and repressed sexual memories of your mother-in-law. *That* guy.

But there's more to the famed psychologist Sigmund Freud than sex and sleep, if you didn't already know. In fact, another important part of Freud's thoughts is his whole idea of the "defense mechanism." These "mechanisms" are a big deal, and can help us, the alcoholics, understand why we lie about what we do.

Let's take a look:

Denial

Denial is the refusal to accept reality or fact. People in denial act as if certain thoughts, emotions, and behaviors simply do not exist. This defense mechanism is clear in early childhood development. Ever heard a kid say, "No I didn't!" when what they did happened right in front of you?

People use denial in their everyday lives to avoid dealing with painful feelings or other things they don't want to face or admit. An alcoholic will say that he or she just likes to drink and doesn't have a problem, even when health is declining, bills are piling up, relationships are struggling, and other clear indicators point to a problem.

If somebody confronts the alcoholic about the problem, the alcoholic may turn the problem on the confronter.

2. Regression

Regression is when we revert to an earlier stage of development amid tough thoughts or negative impulses. For an alcoholic, such earlier stages might be doing nothing but sitting around all day inside, or staying in bed, or refusing to meet adult responsibilities. Instead, the alcoholic will drink and regress, drawing further away from typical mature behaviors that could better the problem.

3. Acting Out

Acting Out is expressing an extreme behavior in order to deal with thoughts or feelings the person could not otherwise express. In place of saying, "You made me mad," a person who acts out may kick a chair, or slam a wall. Children typically have temper tantrums; alcoholics may drink themselves into black-out. They might get in drunken rages, or end up driving recklessly. Bottom line: they're not treating the cause of their emotions.

4. Dissociation

Dissociation is when an individual experiences a change in self- and time- perception. The person is able to find another representation of him or herself in order to continue living without thoughts, feelings or memories that are intolerable. In the mind of the dissociated, time and sense of self do not always flow synchronously; a person who dissociates is essentially disconnecting from the real world. When alcoholics dissociate, they use alcohol to drift away and forget about their worries. Imagine somebody with glassy eyes and an empty bottle, just staring ahead. Completely oblivious.

5. Compartmentalization

Compartmentalization is like dissociation. Compartmentalization is where parts of our consciousness put themselves in separate 'slots,' so to speak. This allows us to separate parts of ourselves that would otherwise cause us great psychological distress. For some people, this may mean being a sleaze ball who bangs hookers on business trips, but then also being a loving father and husband when home. For alcoholics, it could mean driving wasted on weekends at 3 in the morning; and on the other hand, being a law-abiding tax-paying person who doesn't even jaywalk. Individuals who compartmentalize may not even realize the glaring disparity in their attitudes or behaviors. When they do realize, it cause cognitive dissonance, or mental distress caused by contradictory beliefs. In these cases, alcoholics will simply drink to alleviate the uncomfortable feeling.

6. Projection

Projection is when an individual attributes undesired thoughts, feelings or impulses to another person. Sometimes the individual has no idea they're even doing it, especially when that person has little insight into his or her own behaviors. A person may project issues like debt, disease, drug abuse, marital trouble, or any other negative factor.

When alcoholics project, they will label others as alcoholics. Instead of looking at their own drinking habits, they will cite another person who may or may not be just like them. They will accuse alcohol of ruining another person's life in all the same ways that it has ruined theirs. Rarely will they admit that they are equally troubled.

7. Reaction Formation

Reaction Formation is the conversion of negative thoughts, feelings or impulses into their opposite forms. Common examples may include ex-partners acting very nice toward one another when in fact they are very bitter, or employees who hate their bosses but smile and act like all is dandy.

Alcoholics may convince themselves that they are happy when they're actually drinking because they're sad. Alcoholics might also tell themselves that they are sober when they're actually heavily intoxicated.

8. Repression

Repression is the unconscious blocking of certain thoughts, feelings and impulses. Because repressed memories are too difficult to know consciously, they are locked away where they cannot be seen or accessed.

Alcoholics may repress memories that lead to their alcoholism. Alcoholics may also repress memories that occur during their history of alcohol abuse. Anything that can tarnish the mind and body of the alcoholic may end up hidden from thought, without so much as a conscious thought by the individual.

9. Displacement

Displacement is similar to projection. When a person displaces, he or she redirects negative feelings or impulses through an outlet. This means that the individual may feel one way toward a person or object, but instead of taking out those feelings on said person or object, the individual will target something completely different. Classic examples include men who beat their wives due to frustration with work, or people who damage inanimate objects in place of humans.

For the alcoholic, it is common to displace negative emotions on the self. Instead of acting out anger or frustration with a friend, coworker, or lover, the alcoholic will direct emotions inward by drinking heavily to 'self-punish.' The alcoholic may also get involved in domestic abuse.

10. Intellectualization

Intellectualization is the overemphasis on detached and cold thinking in order to deal with a negative aspect of living. Instead of using emotion and reason in balance, the intellectualizer will distance him or herself from the impulse, event or behavior. Intellectualization can be seen in one's words and attitudes, across a variety of contexts. If somebody is dying, the individual may speak of the disease only in terms of facts and statistics, showing little emotion. Regarding the alcoholic, drinking may be self-described in terms of the amount of alcohol consumed, or the frequency of drinking, with little opinion given on the strong emotional component of the disease.

11. Rationalization

Rationalization is used to reframe one's perceptions of what would otherwise be a threatening reality. For instance, a man who lost his job for absenteeism may rationalize his firing as the fault of disorganized management, and not his own doing. An alcoholic who drinks a 30-

pack a day may rationalize such behavior as simply letting loose. Alcoholics love to rationalize. They will find any way to reconceive their destructive drinking and justify their actions. If they do something regrettable while intoxicated, they might rationalize by explaining, "I would have done it either way, drunk or sober" or "Whatever, I was drunk."

12. Undoing

Undoing is the attempt to take back something negative. If you hurt somebody's feelings through selfish acts, you might try to undo it by being very selfless. For alcoholics, acts of undoing might include balancing out a long day of good deeds by getting inebriated, or buying healthy foods to counteract all the money spent on booze. Or working out excessively to sweat out all the booze.

It is all a balancing act.

13. Sublimation

Sublimation is the channeling of unacceptable impulses, thoughts and emotions into appropriate ones. It is considered one of the more adaptive defense mechanisms when used properly. Sublimation typically takes many forms, including humor, fantasizing, and exercise.

For instance, a recovering alcoholic might joke about the stupidity of his actions and even the craziness of his cravings, thus allowing humor to weaken the blow of deeper demons. An alcoholic might also employ fantasy by imagining the end goal of sobriety, even when experiencing setbacks. Many alcoholics also take impulses to drink and get rid of them through rigorous exercise or work.

14. Compensation

Compensation allows the individual to psychologically counterbalance perceived weaknesses by emphasizing other strengths. Thus, the person realistically recognizes that he or she cannot be the best at everything, and that weaknesses in one area do not diminish successes in others.

Alcoholics may use compensation adaptively in order to address issues that lead to drinking. For instance, an alcoholic might realize that he doesn't deal well with daily stressors but is steady like a rock when it comes to life-altering events. Of course, compensation can always run the risk of being *over*-compensation. In such cases, alcoholics may maladaptively appraise strengths and weaknesses: "I'm not the best father, but *man* can I throw back a 30-pack!"

15. Assertiveness

Assertiveness is essentially a balance between being passive and being aggressive. A passive person won't speak up for personal issues but will listen and acquiesce to others. An aggressive person will make personal desires known, but will struggle to listen to others. An assertive person, however, will be direct and clear while also respecting and incorporating the needs and wants of others.

Many alcoholics have trouble finding this balance. They're too aggressive, so they drink to take the edge off. Or they're too passive, so they drink to the point where they don't care anymore. In most cases, alcohol is used to achieve a state that the alcoholic has struggled to reach when sober.

Achieving assertion is a difficult task for many of us, but more so for alcoholics.

All in all, defense mechanism is a difficult beast. The alcoholic will struggle to make sense of everything that has happened. The alcoholic may employ mechanism after mechanism to explain away clearly troubling attitudes and behaviors. In the end, the alcoholic will fall victim to an array of emotional and behavioral problems if defense mechanisms are overused.

Through help from friends, family, and therapists, the alcoholic can learn to recognize negative defense patterns and correct them.

But still, the question remains…

What is an alcoholic? How do we know if defense mechanisms are being used to hide the ugly truth of alcoholism, or if the drinker's thoughts and behaviors are mostly 'normal'?

Again, what… is… alcoholism??

The Alcoholic Brain

Understanding this crazy neural network of ours is never an easy task. Fortunately, there are very smart people hard at work on the mission. When assessing whether you or someone you know is an alcoholic, it is important to realize the complexity of the diagnosis. But even more, it is important to realize the complexity of the human brain.

Why can some people enjoy alcohol for a while and suffer no repercussions? Why does another person take a sip of a beer and suddenly they're drinking 15 beers a day for 20 years? Is it the environment? Is it the way people are raised, fashioned by a certain system of beliefs and values? Is it mostly genetic, the unpreventable result of strange permutations in our DNA sequences and expressions?

What in the world causes some people to fall completely apart while others can drink over and over without a single problem in sight?

One of the leading problems is obviously culture itself. In fact, studies show that the United States has the highest rate of binge-drinking among teens, with American teens far more likely to be killed by violence than peers in Europe. Because substance dependence is shown to be more likely when drinking starts early in development, it is no surprise that a good portion of these American teens end up dependent upon alcohol.

In fact, an estimated 17 million Americans have what is medically termed an "alcohol use disorder." Each year in the U.S., nearly 80,000 people die from alcohol-related causes, with 1,825 college students between the ages of 18 and 24 dying from alcohol-related unintentional injuries such as car crashes.

Alcohol is clearly everywhere. By age 15, more than 50 percent of teens have had at least 1 drink, and more adolescents drink alcohol than smoke cigarettes or use marijuana.

So then how the heck can we distinguish an alcoholic from anybody else? If college kids and teenagers and even older children are getting their hands on the sauce, isn't all this talk of alcoholism just redundant?

Heck, from the looks of things, one might think we're a *global society* of alcoholics.

And maybe we are…

Still, we have to start somewhere. People who can drink responsibly should be allowed to do so, just as people who don't should be restricted. When a drinker's alcohol use is interfering with important aspects of his or her life—as well as in others' lives—then we've got a problem.

In order to diagnose that problem, we have the Diagnostic and Statistical Manual of Mental Disorders (the DSM-V). Although the fifth edition of this manual is just one form of guidelines, it is considered the premiere reference in psychiatry and psychology.

Developed by the American Psychiatric Association, the DSM-V covers all mental health disorders for both children and adults, listing known causes of disorders, statistics in terms of gender, age at onset and prognosis, and research concerning the best treatment approaches.

The DSM is typically considered the 'bible' for any professional who makes psychiatric diagnoses in the United States and other modern countries. In terms of alcoholism, the DSM-V is especially important. Alcoholic tendencies associated with obtaining and using alcohol are now categorized under one "use disorder." Depending on the amount of matching symptoms, "Alcohol Use Disorder" can occur as mild, moderate or severe. The presence of 2 to 3 is considered mild; 4 to 5, moderate; and 6 or more, severe.

The symptoms are:

1. Taking the substance in larger amounts or for longer than the

you meant to

2. Wanting to cut down or stop using the substance but not managing to

3. Spending a lot of time getting, using, or recovering from use of the substance

4. Cravings and urges to use the substance

5. Not managing to do what you should at work, home or school, because of substance use

6. Continuing to use, even when it causes problems in relationships

7. Giving up important social, occupational or recreational activities because of substance use

8. Using substances again and again, even when it puts the you in danger

9. Continuing to use, even when the you know you have a physical or psychological problem that could have been caused or made worse by the substance

10. Needing more of the substance to get the effect you want (tolerance)

11. Development of withdrawal symptoms, which can be relieved by taking more of the substance.

Again, you might be scratching your head. The words used as 'criteria' can be vague and are almost always dependent upon a variety of factors—one of which is the subjective interpretation of the specialist. The interpretations of family, friends, and patients are also important. If disagreement occurs, it is often up to a combination of consensus and presiding medical opinion to pin down the diagnosis. Without various opinions, the disorder might be assigned too hastily, or in other cases, not at all.

Fortunately, there are other indicators. The National Epidemiological Study on Alcohol and Related Conditions has shown that more than 70 percent of people with alcohol dependence have a single episode that lasts roughly 3 or 4 years. To the alcoholic, it may just be business as usual. Another minute, another drink. But to outsiders, this 3-4 year period is clearly a new low in the alcoholic's life. The self-destruction is clear. The spiraling of the alcoholic is clear. The alcoholic's unwillingness to stop is clear.

If you're like me, you can have all the indicators right in front of your face exploding like a supernova, but you still won't notice. If you're like me, you need to hear the same thing over and over; you need to fuck up again and again; you need to see your loved ones crying in court, staring at you with their wearied eyes through the other side of a prison phone booth. You need to see that fading trust, and the disappearance of friends and foes, like ghosts.

If you're like me, you need the same thing said again, but differently. You need the same core message hammered home with a new nail.

The National Institute on Alcohol Abuse and Alcoholism (NIAAA) has provided a helpful set of questions. They're similar to other criteria, but worded slightly differently. Check all that have occurred in the past year:

Top of Form

had times when you ended up drinking **more, or longer,** than you

intended?

more than once wanted to **cut down or stop** drinking, or tried to,

but couldn't?

more than once gotten into situations while or after drinking that **increased**

your chances of getting hurt (such as driving, swimming, using machinery, walking in a dangerous area, or having unsafe sex)?

had to drink **much more** than you once did to **get the effect** you want?

Or found that your **usual number** of drinks had **much less effect** than

before?

continued to drink even though it was making you feel **depressed or**

anxious or adding to **another health problem**?

Or after having had a **memory blackout**?

spent a **lot of time** drinking? Or being sick or getting over other after

effects?

continued to drink even though it was causing **trouble** with

your **family** or **friends**?

found that drinking—or being sick from drinking—often **interfered**

with taking care of your **home** or **family**?

Or caused **job** troubles? Or **school** problems?

given up or **cut back** on **activities** that were important or interesting

to you, or gave you pleasure, in order to drink?

more than once gotten **arrested,** been held at a police station, or

had other **legal problems** because of your drinking?

found that when the effects of alcohol were wearing off, you

had **withdrawal symptoms,** such as trouble sleeping, shakiness,

restlessness, nausea, sweating, a racing heart, or a seizure?

Or sensed things that were not there?

Okay, so now you might have a *slightly* better idea of where you stand. Hopefully you are approaching a more honest appraisal of your condition or the condition of somebody you know. If anything, you've at least learned *something*.

Or perhaps you're drunk right now, and won't remember reading any of this. In which case, I think you might have a problem…

Regardless, we still have ground to cover. What brings on alcoholism? What does the science, the literature, say about the onset of alcohol dependence in individuals?

What do the experts with the big foreheads and research studies say about the alcoholic's suffering?

Science of Alcoholism

The addict's biggest problem is the chronic nature of addiction. Because the brain has literally rearranged its connections, it is very difficult to change them back. This takes time, and at any point *during* that time, the alcoholic is susceptible to relapse. Sometimes, after years of abuse, many neurons may be permanently gone. It may take years for the brain to restore itself to 'normal' functioning.

And only one shot of Whiskey to lose it all again…

So then what causes it?

I don't know, and neither do most people. I mean, I kinda know—I *am* an alcoholic after all.

Well I guess I should clarify. I am a *recovering* alcoholic after all.

Scientists and researchers talk about alcoholism like they would most diseases or disorders. Basically, it is largely explained by the craziness of the human brain. Environment, circumstance and genetics all factor into this equation.

When it comes to the human brain, the reward pathway is the central mechanism responsible for turning some people into alcoholics and leaving others acting normally. When you ingest alcohol, this so-called reward pathway gets excited. Because it is tied to most areas of the brain, the excitement of drinking alcohol is then reinforced in memory, movement, and motivation, among other areas.

The chemicals that cause this excitement are called neurotransmitters. Neurotransmitters are released in high levels when we drink, explaining why drinking can feel *sooo* good. In fact, the amount of the neurotransmitter dopamine released by drugs of abuse can be two to ten times higher than the amount released by natural pleasures, like delicious food. The effects of drugs and alcohol also last a lot longer, making them very addictive.

The effect of high levels of dopamine on the brain is so powerful that the brain must learn to adapt, to regulate. Because the brain cannot sustain such high levels, it desensitizes itself by reducing the amount of neurotransmitters released. Thus, with continued drinking, we need more and more to achieve the same level of intoxication. Basically, this is called "tolerance." The more often you drink, the more desensitized your receptors become and the more alcohol you need to feel great.

When we get used to needing that 'great' feeling, we become addicted. The neurons in our brain that release neurotransmitters become dependent on the drug. The brain will no longer produce or release the neurotransmitters that make us feel pleasure by itself. Because the brain can no longer bring pleasure without alcohol, the alcoholic feels depressed and unable to experience pleasure in activities that used to be enjoyable. As a result, the user experiences withdrawal symptoms when the drug is not in their system. At this point, it's no longer a matter of craving alcohol to get drunk.

It's about *needing* alcohol just to feel 'normal.'

Researchers have found that alcoholism is greatly influenced by certain genes. In fact, genetic factors make up *40 to 60 percent* of the differences between alcoholics and non-alcoholics. The genes involved in susceptibility to alcoholism include alcohol-specific genes and those that impact pathways affecting reward, behavioral control and stress management. Stress actually plays a major role, with as many as 45% of alcoholic patients also meeting the diagnostic criteria for anxiety disorders.

When it comes to alcoholism and our genes, the underlying causes go deep. Genetic predisposition to addiction occurs not only due to genetic sequences, but also due to genetic expressions. Changes in specific genetic expressions are inheritable and lay the groundwork for the study of "epigenetics."

In short, epigenetics is the study of how unique chemical reactions activate and deactivate pieces of the genome at specific times and locations. Epigenetics is the meticulous breakdown of these chemical reactions and the factors that influence them.

Basically, our genes have countless tags that turn certain functions on and off. These tags represent all the signals the cell has received in its lifetime. In this sense, the cells have very real memories. *Cellular memory.*

Like our memories, our cells' memories are constantly changing depending upon environmental and internal factors. Exercise, diet, and interpersonal experiences all create signals that travel from cell to cell throughout our bodies. Signals from within the body are invaluable when it comes to physical growth and learning. Just look at what happens during puberty!

Environmental signals change cells so that they can respond to changes in the outside world. Internal signals deliver maintenance to bodily processes, like rejuvenating blood cells and skin, and fixing damaged tissues and organs. During these processes, cellular memories activate and deactivate specific genes.

Although it may take many generations for a genetic trait to gain traction in a population, our epigenome can change rapidly. Through epigenetic inheritance, experiences of parents may pass to children. Epigenetic inheritance may permit an organism to constantly change its expression to match its environment—without ever changing the actual DNA code.

Still, researchers are now growing more confident about certain genes that may trigger alcoholism." A 2004 study in the journal *Alcoholism: Clinical and Experimental Research* was the first to demonstrate an association between GABA, a major neurotransmitter, and alcoholism. The study focused on 262 families, a total of 2,282 individuals, and found that one receptor for GABA, Gabrg3, correlated strongly with alcohol dependence.

Other studies in more recent years have also linked genes to alcoholism. One new study has shown that normal mice show no interest in alcohol and drink little or no alcohol when offered a free choice between water and diluted alcohol. However, mice with a genetic mutation of another GABA receptor, Gabrb1, chose alcohol over water with tremendous regularity. In fact, these mice consumed nearly 85% of their daily fluid as drinks containing as much alcohol as wine.

But this is no surprise. Numerous animal studies demonstrate that alcohol-related characteristics like intoxication sensitivity, sedative effects, tolerance/withdrawal cycles, and susceptibility to organ damage all have genetic sources.

The genetic component of alcoholism is undoubtedly gaining more traction in the literature. Because gene mutations are passed down, alcohol dependence has a very strong heredity component, giving credence to the saying, "We're a family of drunks!"

Of course, it can go both ways. Some genetic mutations make others less likely to become addicted or even enjoy alcohol. An example would be people of Asian descent. Because people of Asian descent have a gene variant that changes their rate of alcohol metabolism, they often experience flushing, nausea, and rapid heartbeat when drinking. Effects like this make alcohol use very tough for said individuals, helping to protect them from developing alcoholism.

Unfortunately, alcoholics are not nearly so lucky. Addicts become obsessed with their behaviors and ignore the life-threatening consequences. Many experts now agree that addiction is essentially an imbalance between the neural system that is reactive for signaling pain or pleasure and another neural system that reflects and controls that system.

In studies of non-addicts, the ventromedial prefontal cortex (VMPC) is an important part of the brain controlling decision making. When injured, these non-addicts make poor decisions and fail to learn from mistakes; their post-injury personality starkly contrasts with their pre-injury personality.

Just like VMPC patients, addicts have trouble seeing problems and consequences. They become less likely to reflect and choose wisely, and generally move from self-directed behavior to automatic, sensory-driven behavior. Addiction becomes a battle between *right now* and *later on*. As long as the addict can get that fix in the moment, what happens after doesn't matter.

Although addicts *use* in order to numb the moment and ignore the future, the past is not forgotten. In fact, memories of use are often easily retrievable during periods of "craving" and may lead to immediate relapse. Meanwhile, memories of successful sobriety and recently learned behaviors are not stored or retrieved with the same ease.

The addict often fails to remember other rewarding experiences that could replace or diminish the primary addiction. Even if they do remember, addicts rarely make the investment necessary for such rewarding pursuits. More often than not, the addict maintains a partial consciousness of the destructive and alienating waves of their addiction. In most cases, the individual only enters treatment as a result of some consequence of use like relationship trouble or job issues, and rarely due to a new insight into personal addiction.

Sobriety is a perpetual struggle. Addicts will suffer from "post-acute withdrawal" early on in their sobriety, typically experiencing concentration issues, irritability, and insomnia. When the feeling of discomfort arrives, the addict is accustomed to using.

When that impulsive craving rears its ugly head, physiological, psychological, and social aid become necessary. Education is also necessary, but by itself will not change the addict. The intellectual effects of education are not enough to change the physiological changes caused by drugs.

The good news out of all of this is that most people are not alcoholics. The majority of people out at bars, drinking with dinner, enjoying wine with lunch, are not addicted to alcohol, even though they might very much enjoy it. Moreover, the overwhelming majority of these people will not *become* addicted to alcohol.

That said, the difference between these people and me, between these people and perhaps *you*, is no different than any *other* difference. Just like some people can never work out and look great whereas other people can bust their ass and never lose weight—it's the same thing. Just like people are different athletes or students or thinkers or doers or—you name it.

With everything, it is hard to know what the biggest factor is. Is it because of how we were born? Is it more because of the circumstances we've endured, or the environment we've been a part of? Is it due to the way we act in the moment, in the fray?

What causes *what* and *when*?

Nobody can say absolutely, but at the very least, the image is becoming clearer. Less haze, less fuzz—which is a good thing. So choose clarity over depravity. Remove your booze goggles and see the world through the world's eyes.

My Personal Journey

I remember sitting in an AA meeting one fall evening, thinking to myself "what a waste of fucking time."

I was younger, surrounded by sad, haggard men and women twice my age. As I peered around the room, making sure to keep my head low, I saw what I wanted to see. I saw people who were not like me. People who were worn down and beaten up, the kind of drawn, tired people who could do nothing but lament their many mistakes.

One guy would always speak of how his wife had left him. Another woman talked about sucking back pints of vodka every day, how she used to show up to business luncheons wasted off her ass. How she showed up to *everything* wasted off her ass.

I remember wondering how these people lived life outside of meetings. I couldn't help but imagine that they *didn't* live life outside of meetings; that their lives were merely a grey world of AA and NA cults; of sad stories and blown chances.

"I'm not like these pathetic saps," I told myself. "I'm just a kid. I'm just a fuckin kid enjoying life, and nobody, no freaking druggie or drunk, is gonna tell me to stop."

Except I wasn't enjoying life.

From a young age I was always detached, trying to make sense of the way the world seemed to move by me. Time was like a heavy fog to me, and the only way to see through was through the clarity of an empty bottle.

Booze, beer, wine, absinthe—it didn't matter. What mattered was that I keep it going. Because when it stopped, when life came to a screeching, sober halt…

I might as well have been dead.

I had a gift that I recognized from an early age. Unlike most people, I didn't need to connect. A lot of people I knew sought companionship. They formed circles of friends, acquaintances; a person for this interest, a group for that.

People had boyfriends and girlfriends, fiancées and "soul mates." By and large, people seemed to have it all figured out.

But maybe they didn't. Maybe they were weak, and I was the strong one. Maybe I was the strong one because I didn't need *anybody*. As long as I had my alcohol, all of that other shit didn't matter.

So many days I spent just driving around, me and my booze. I'd drive for hours, no direction or destination, nothing but the gradually increasing buzz.

But there was part of me that wanted that connection. Somewhere inside my weakening heart, I had an incredible capacity for love—and many days, I wondered if anybody cared. Or even knew.

A couple days a week I would stop by the grocery store. Like anything I did, I couldn't be out and about without having *something* in me. In my mind, it was all too easy. I would adjust my seat, kick back with the handle in my hands, and drain down the sauce.

"Just a couple more guzzles and then you can go in," I'd tell myself.

Except, it was never just a couple more guzzles. I'd spend so much time watching people walk by my car with their carts and groceries; with friends and family. I'd spend minute after minute getting wasted, in my car, in the parking lot of a grocery store.

Maybe it was early evening. Maybe it was 1, 2, or 3 in the afternoon. Or maybe it was noon, or 10 am.

It didn't matter what it was. It didn't matter if I was supposed to be at work. None of that mattered to me.

Sitting around and drinking, and watching through the looking-glass—

that's what mattered. Most times I barely made it out of my car. Instead, I'd fire up the engine and continue my journey on the way to nowhere.

Many mornings I'd wake up forgetting how I got home. Who I talked to. Where I'd been.

Most of the time, I woke up alone.

For a period of years, I told myself that I was going to find a woman. I was an attractive man by others' estimations, but I rarely saw it. Time and time again women would look at me, with this look. Like they were trying to figure me out; like they wanted to know me.

It never made sense—why would anybody want to *know* me?

I had friends that loved to drink, but not like me. Most times when I went out, I went out by myself. I'd wander the bars, ordering the cheapest and the strongest, occasionally disappearing to the parking lot to chug down my own stash. Or to smoke a bowl. Or to snort a line.

Anything that could bring me where I wanted to go—which was never close enough.

I kept this up for a while, and some nights I'd get lucky. Cute ladies would brush up against me. They'd flick their hair, they'd purse their lips, they'd search my glassy eyes with that submissive feminine gaze that men just love.

Maybe they saw the sadness in my eyes, my features. Maybe they wanted to help, to feel what I felt. Or maybe they were just looking.

For me, it didn't matter. One-night stands were all that mattered, and when the deed was done, I was gone. No phone number, no morning after—nothing.

Some people thought that having sex with a woman and then sneaking out in the early morning was a terrible thing.

But this never made sense to me.

The terrible thing, I thought, was to stay. Because when morning rolled around, and sobriety took its hold, she would finally know. She would realize the truth: that I was a nobody.

That I was poor, pathetic, and heartless. And I couldn't do that to a woman—to anybody. I couldn't dare open up to anybody.

Even through DUIs and public intoxication and assault and resisting arrest, I continued to justify my actions. Sometimes I swore my head was clear, and I'd *know* that it was all figured out.

I'd test myself, having no more than 5 or 6 drinks at the bar and then leaving. For a while, I pulled this off. I was in control, I was successful.

Alcoholics couldn't do this, I'd tell myself. Therefore, I was not an alcoholic. The inpatient and outpatient recoveries, the weekend interventions, the 28-day rehabilitations, the transitional housing, the courts, the friends, the family—all of them were wrong. Only *I* could know who I was and what I was.

Alcoholics were one thing. And I sure as hell wasn't one of 'em. Besides, what gave anybody the right to tell me I was "addicted" to anything? It was such a stupid conception.

I wasn't just arguing semantics; I was being truthful.

Technically people could get "addicted" to coffee. To sex, and exercise, and shopping, and eating, and videogames, and being lazy, worthless *fucks*. So then why in the hell was my love for drinking somehow an "addiction," yet all that other crap was fine?

Everybody telling me that I had a problem was a fuckin hypocrite. *They* were the ones with the problem. *They* were the ones in denial, the ones who couldn't see the world for the way it really was.

Not me—never me.

But soon the doubts started creeping in. I floated between having confidence to thinking nothing of myself. It was a constant struggle for balance and sometimes the scale would tip so far in one direction, I swore I was falling off the side of the Earth.

Still, time and time again, I dragged myself back. One hand on the spinning ground, one hand on the bottle, I'd right myself just enough.

Jobs came and went, friends came and went, and the only thing that stayed was the sauce. When I thought about it, I realized that the only thing I had ever truly trusted in my life was the sauce. It was my steady rock; my dependable friend.

People, I thought, came with motives and agendas. But the bottle, the sauce, didn't judge. It didn't care if you were a 24-year-old hotshot or a grizzled geezer. The sauce would deliver regardless.

Sometimes I would reflect on my life, especially when I was unemployed. Days would pass with drunk considerations of my meaning; my purpose in this grand game.

Many mornings I wondered if my "loved ones" actually loved me.

I thought about relationships. Girls who had left me and were now married or posing in pictures with their significant others, soaking up sun in their newfound happiness.

I thought about treatment programs, court sentences, AA and NA meetings. I mulled over the words of the wise and the knowing. For a while I even entertained the idea that maybe they were right.

Because perhaps, a part of that poor sap in my AA class was also a part of me.

From time to time I'd receive missed calls or get texts from former friends. Some of them were girls who seemed to really care. "How are you?" they'd ask. "It's been a while."

"I hope you're okay," some would say.

I didn't know what to say so I usually said nothing. You're out of my life now, I'd think. So *fuck* you.

Or maybe they were right. Was it possible that their concern was warranted? That I really was a person in need of saving? That maybe I actually *deserved* a guardian angel?

Was I any different than all the other drunks and deadbeats?

But soon I'd forget, or deny. It only took one day for the drink to come back in my brain. And despite it all, despite the poison that was ruining everything I had ever done, the drink always made me smile. It was almost too good to be legal.

There you are, old friend. It's good to feel you once again.

I wasn't depressed and I didn't need help. I was living life the way I chose to live it, and it was no business of other people's. They had their own shit to worry about—why they would worry about me was *beyond* me.

All I wanted was to go unbothered.

"I'm attending classes and staying sober," I'd say to the judge. And by nighttime I was drunk.

"I'm doing everything right, staying out of trouble," I'd tell my parole officer, hoping that she wouldn't be testing my urine; praying to the god I wasn't sure existed, that the altoids in my mouth hid the alcohol on my breath.

"One drink is too many and a thousand not enough," this man in my AA used to say. It never made sense in the early years, but as time passed, wisdom grew. And with something like a million drinks of experience, those hoarse words from an old man finally touched home.

In the end, it was the shared experience that brought me to sobriety. All the jail time and financial trouble and broken relationships in the world wouldn't change me, until I accepted who I was.

I wasn't *better* than these other people. We were all struggling, all fighting to find our way in this wide world, in the time we had. No matter what I said, it was the words of others, speaking for me, that spoke most to my soul.

Alcoholics Anonymous was not some cult, like I used to believe. It was not a collection of worthless low-lifes fucked up beyond repair. It wasn't a death sentence and it wasn't a condemnation.

By the end, and the start (of sobriety), I learned something. I realized that I actually *did* care. That there was nothing criminal in *feeling* life. I learned that I didn't have to be a religious zealot or a zombie to move through life without the sauce.

I realized that I could approach every moment and every day with the same fervor I put into drinking. I learned to be happy in the small things, to worry less and love more; to be a person that people could look to. To be source of strength, to be a confidante, to be a friend and a lover, and a world of difference in a world so difficult.

And it was amazing.

I don't read the Bible, I used to think. *I don't follow the 10 Commandments, and I'm sure as hell not following the 12 steps.* In my opening years of AA, I didn't care. If you had asked me which one of the steps I was working through, I couldn't have told you. "Pick one," I might have said. "It's all bullshit anyway."

One of the members, this woman who looked nothing the part of a booze hound, used to talk. She volunteered to share virtually every meeting, and as I started attending more and more, I recognized just how crazy her life was.

When she talked, she spoke of things in terms that I could understand. "Think how lucky we are," she used to say. "People with diabetes—do they have meetings like this?"

Many people with other diseases did not have the opportunity to openly share. They had to tend to their problems in relative isolation. They didn't know what it was like to absorb the lessons of others just like them. There were no daily meetings, no weekend functions.

There was no AA equivalent for a lot of people in a lot of conditions. In many ways, AA was an animal all its own. A unique mix of anecdote, testimony, and structure. That woman with the 23 years of sobriety was right.

It was the first time I had ever thought of myself as "lucky."

Finding Success in Treatment

Over time, as the brain is forced to continue to adapt to alcohol or drugs, the other areas of the brain outside the reward pathway become affected. The circuitry of the brain that is responsible for memory, learning and judgment becomes hardwired to perform addictive behavior almost innately. It disrupts crucial brain structures that are critical for controlling behavior, especially behaviors related specifically to alcohol or drugs. It erodes one's ability to display self-control and make good decisions. Thus, the drug user is now the drug addict. The drinker, now fallen from the wagon.

But this is why we have treatment. This is the reasoning behind clinics and interventions and therapy sessions. Because alcohol changes our brain, we have no choice but to fight it with everything we've got.

Personally, I never liked self-diagnosis. Once I decided that I wanted to stop drinking, I didn't care what it was called. Whether or not I was "allergic" to alcohol, "dependent" on alcohol, "addicted" to alcohol, "powerless" over alcohol—it didn't matter. At the final stage, all I wanted was to progress. The only thing I needed to do was to keep doing whatever I *could* do aside from drinking.

So I started looking over the steps. This time, I came with fresh eyes and a clear mind. I still didn't care so much for the whole concept of "GOD," but I knew that that wasn't what mattered. Somehow, being around these other people was beginning to help.

Psychiatrists might have called this group therapy, or interpersonal therapy. But for me, I just called it talking. Just hanging out, hanging around, shooting the shit and talking life with people who in many ways knew me better than my own family.

Not all AA meetings helped; some were terrible. It took me years to find a home group and a sponsor, but it eventually panned out. Once I stopped going to the 'exorcism' meetings rife with people crying for you to "release your demons," I learned something—there's a group for everyone.

I found the people I wanted to be, the people who made me feel good and feel bad and feel everything from shit to sunshine. I enjoyed being around people who allowed me to confront my emotions and my fears—and I, rather assuredly, helped them do the same.

They genuinely cared too. And it was genuine—I knew it was—because they had all been there. Maybe not exactly, perhaps not for the same reasons, but still… they had all been in the trenches.

When a woman broke down in tears because she had lost custody of her kids, I was there. When a man celebrated his 2nd decade of sobriety, I was there. When a mother and son duo entered their first AA meeting, I was there. When a member was finally able to admit to the group a vehicular manslaughter from 30 years prior, I was there.

I began to realize that this was part of my reason for being here. *Here*, in this crazy world. But I also realized that AA wasn't for everybody. Some people were just fine doing whatever worked for them. There were plenty of people who could hit the switch, and kick the habit. One day a daily drinker of 25 years, and then flash forward: 25 years of sobriety with a family and a 401k; sipping mojitos in the Caribbean.

Life could always turn around—something I had, for the majority of my life, disbelieved. The way we turned it around depended upon the need for change: the *need* for being stronger than we gave ourselves credit for.

Because we all are—stronger, that is. Everybody I have ever met, and everybody you have ever met, has the potential to deal with shit. Life will throw us shit and we can sink in it without our shoes, or we can step above it. Hell, we can even use it as fertilizer.

For me, it was always about self-education. I started reading more. I used to read all the time, before alcohol and drugs, but that wonderful habit disappeared amid the haze.

Fortunately, when the fog lifted, I was able to pour myself back into the information. The internet taught me so many things, books at my local library taught me so many things—everywhere I looked, I looked to learn.

I learned about self-confidence, and trust, and neurochemistry, and genetics, and heredity, and addiction, and pharmacology, and existence, and everything everywhere that could make me understand why I was the way I was.

I am by no means an 'expert,' but in many ways I think that's a good thing. I've been through things that I daresay many researchers, psychologists and psychiatrists have not. They may have studied these things ad nauseam, but do they know what it's like from the other side?

Do they know what it's like to be hopelessly hooked?

Have they gone day after day, blacking out, fighting and battling those who loved them, people who had made every sacrifice to change their ways? Have they shown up to treatment classes, only to be denied at the door because they failed the breathalyzer?

Have they ever been so wasted and dependent upon alcohol that they actually lapped up their own vomit, thinking it could get them drunker?

When I look back at my life, there are a lot of memories. But there are also a lot of times that I can't recall. When I think about it now, I wonder how much time I lost.

How many days were spent in auto-pilot, my brain literally swimming in alcohol?

To this day, I continue to share with AA the trials and tribulations of my course. My *trajectory*—if you want to call it that. Although I will admit that the 12-steps can be very difficult at times, I stick to them because they've finally started working. Because, as my sponsor often says, "it works if you work it."

Even so, there are plenty of people who will tell you it doesn't work. These people come from a variety of walks of life, and if it doesn't work for them, it doesn't work for them. They are neither 'right' nor 'wrong.' Maybe they haven't given it the chance it deserves, or possibly they've poured themselves into it, and have found little success.

The point is simple: we are all different. Because we are all different, we will all find different ways of fighting our vices and our addictions.

According to the author of _Breaking Addiction_, Lance Dodes, the body of research now approximates the success rate of AA at somewhere between 5 and 10 percent. In Dodes' opinion, AA has probably the worst success rate in all of medicine. He argues that AA actually harms people because for the 90-95% who are unsuccessful, AA is expressed as *the* treatment for alcoholism. Thus, if you fail in AA, it is not AA that has failed. It is you.

Dodes believes that AA works for the people it does because it forms a brotherhood; camaraderie. Basically, Dodes finds no use for the 12-steps, explaining that the support and structure of AA is what leads to success, not the series of bible-like guidelines.

Frankly, I have no problem with this. It doesn't matter to me if what works for you, doesn't work for more. I encourage you to concoct your own treatment program, to seek the people and resources that help you. I don't necessarily believe that people who don't benefit from AA are somehow worse off than had they never attended AA at all.

I understand that Dodes may be implying that people who don't stop drinking as a result of AA may then internalize their failure and drink more. However, I would argue that these people were already drinking heavily prior to attending AA, and that it is their psychological and physical constitutions that are the source of relapse, and not failure in

AA.

They 'fail' in AA not because they are failures but because their specific constitution does not respond to AA. This does not mean that other sources of treatment will not work more effectively. Personally, I've met people who quit AA and went through treatment programs and clinics and got sober that way. For me, these treatment programs and clinics did nothing, and it was AA that ultimately worked.

Or perhaps it was simply the cumulative effects of all these powerful pressures, repaving my path.

To each his or her own, I say.

Still, I want to explain how I navigate the 12-steps, as I feel that Dodes thinks very little of them. Let's go through them one by one, and maybe this will help:

Step 1: "We admitted we were powerless over alcohol, that our lives had become unmanageable."

Honestly, this is often the hardest. Some people just don't quite get the wording, which was where I stood. "Powerless," you say?

What hell is that? For the longest time, I didn't want to admit that I couldn't control drinking. I figured I just liked it and liked to do whatever I wanted to do. Had that landed me in trouble? Yes. Was I using and abusing other drugs? Yes. Was I losing my family and friends, my health and my career? Yes.

Sure, maybe you could have convinced me that my life was *becoming* "unmanageable," but the world "powerless" just didn't apply.

That made me feel weak and foolish. It sounded like I had no power at all, which was utter bullshit. Of course I had power. At the very least, I had the power to pick up a drink. I had the power to do what I wanted, when I wanted. Sure, occasionally the State would take that power away, but it would always come back.

No matter how bad I fucked up, I had a way of coming back.

But then I realized something. Admitting being "powerless" did not mean I was admitting being powerless over everything, forever.

And forget the word powerless. It wasn't about power, it was about my life. I simply wanted something to stick to, something to believe in. Many members at AA openly admitted that they didn't stick to the Steps word for word. Like anything, they interpreted those words differently, and aligned them to fit with their plan. When I finally started reading and considering the steps, I had already devised my plan.

I had formed my narrative, and when I started integrating with society (perhaps for the first time, truly), I learned what to say. I still go to bars today, with mostly new people. Most of my old friends are forgotten friends. Some are dead.

Do I miss them from time to time? Yes and no. Do I miss drinking?

I would be disingenuous if I said I never missed certain instances of drinking. But I don't miss drinking in general. And I certainly don't miss all the shit it made me go through. I feel so much better today— hell, I even feel happy. Granted, I used a lot of different *stuff* other than alcohol, so I know that quitting that shit too has made a big difference.

Still, it's so much better sober. Life, I mean. When people ask if I drink, I tell them I don't. If they ask why, which they often do, I tell them that I can't control it. Most of the time, they respect this. The words "powerless" or "unmanageable" rarely come up.

Step 2: "Came to believe that a Power greater than ourselves could restore us to sanity."

This was another really hard one for me. Mainly because I didn't believe in God and thought that "Power greater than ourselves" was pretty much saying "Believe in God, buddy."

I didn't like that. It bothered me that I would have to believe in God. Okay, so let's say I now believe in God. Now what? What has that done? Some dude on a cloud is watching over me, and feels bad for me, of all 8 billion people or whatever?

Oh wait, so when I don't believe in him, he doesn't give a shit about me? But all of a sudden, once I start kneeling before him he'll give two shits?

I'm still not sure if I believe in God to this day, but I do believe in a sense of meaning. I believe that there is a connection between people, but I don't know what to call it.

If you call that God, *great*. But I don't. For now, I will just call it what the step vaguely calls it, "Power greater than ourselves." To me, this power is the power of people. I believe that Step 2 is about looking outside yourself. It's about realizing that people around you can help you if you let them in, at least a bit.

Has getting sober restored me to sanity? I'm not sure if I've ever been sane, and neither is my family, but I would say that I *feel* better. I generally and specifically feel better, and everything we know about science, the body and the mind tells me that I *should* feel better.

Step 3: "Made a decision to turn our will and our lives over to the care of God as we understood God."

In case you didn't know, Alcoholics Anonymous was founded as a religious organization whose members believed strongly in the purging of sinfulness through conversion experiences. Even today, the biblical 'Big Book' is the sobriety guide lauded by members.

Again, I tend to keep my thinking secular and pragmatic. I don't worry too much about religion, I worry about changing my life. One of the members once told me that "God" for him was never God. "God" was "Good, orderly direction."

For me, this is a euphemism. I simply got tired of things and realized that I needed to get my shit together. Good, orderly direction was another way of saying "time to stop fucking up."

Because that's what it really was. I was destroying myself and those I loved. I was hurting people one by one, and making everybody feel shitty. I was being selfish and self-hating; I had no reason to live most days, and maybe part of me was hoping I'd slip up one night when wasted and end it all. I dunno.

What I did know was that I wanted to feel like I could walk a higher path. I wanted to make others feel good, because then I would feel good. I wanted to make myself feel good, so I was in a position to make others feel good.

Some may argue that this step makes it seem like the power to change resides in a spiritual being and not in the addict. I feel like it's both. I came to AA and therefore I saw the 12-steps, posted and displayed for all to see on faded yellow parchment. I learned about the 12-steps because I, myself, decided to give a shot, to show up physically to the building, to move my eyes to that list of steps, and to read left to right those bolded words.

Maybe some higher power was compelling me, maybe we were symbiotic—I don't know. What I do know is that a thought occurred in my head one day and I decided enough was enough. Whether that thought was planted there by a supreme force or being, I can't say.

But I will say that I'm sober today.

Step 4: "Made a searching and fearless moral inventory of ourselves."

This step will anger some because it seems to imply that our addiction to alcohol is a moral quandary, not a scientific disease.

But can't it be both? I mean, people acquire diseases because they sometimes abuse things, right? Sure, some people just seem to have it—but a lot of alcoholics will tell you that they started as normal drinkers. Perhaps this is self-denial, but in many regards it is not.

You will hear of drinkers who started when friends did, in high school or college. For the longest time, they were able to enjoy alcohol without issues. Then they continued to press, continued to go further, knowing that nothing bad had happened yet.

Similarly, people may develop high blood pressure, or heart disease, or liver problems, or cancer, or even contract viruses, all because of what they did. Is it not a moral problem if somebody smokes 2 packs a day and gets cancer, or abuses candy and gets diabetes? If we define moral as a matter of 'good' and 'bad,' is it not useful to look inward to see what we don't like about ourselves and our past?

Diseases and illnesses are sometimes brought on by doing things that most people would consider 'bad.' That doesn't mean we can't still conceptualize the problem as a disease or illness or disorder. It just means that this problem may be caused by an inability or unwillingness to look inward and address it.

Drinking, eating, smoking, exercising, stressing, and sleeping too much can all contribute to problems. Just as doing too little of something can lead to problems. Living life at the fringe of extremity can be fatal.

When we take "moral inventory," we at least think about ourselves and these problems. Being fearless about them helps even more—well, for me.

When I looked inward, I was no longer suppressing my issues. I couldn't keep ignoring them, and I couldn't keep lying to myself. It was extremely tough at first to be honest with myself, but it ultimately worked. From fearful to fearless.

And for that I am happy.

Step 5: "Admitted to God, to ourselves, and to another human being the exact nature of our wrongs."

Step 6: "Were entirely ready to have God remove all these defects of character."

Step 7: "Humbly asked God to remove our shortcomings."

Again, the word "God" comes up in these three steps, which made them really tough for me initially. I finally learned that once I admitted alcoholism to myself, I was in fact admitting to good, orderly direction as well. Hearing the voices dance in my head as I talked to my conscience, felt like I was connecting. The hardest part was admitting to another person what I had done wrong.

In asking "God" to remove my defects and shortcomings, I essentially submitted to the existence of possibility. That is, I finally acknowledged that it was possible for me to improve my life and the lives of others; that I wasn't just some person who would *never* figure it out. I spoke to myself, I examined my thoughts, and I thought about how this could change my attitudes and behaviors for the better. This may sound like a load of bullshit, but it's actually kind of the premise of cognitive behavioral therapy (CBT), one of the leading therapy styles for addicts today.

Step 8: "Made a list of all persons we had harmed and became willing to make amends to them all."

Step 9: "Made direct amends to such people wherever possible, except when to do so would injure them or others."

If, like me, you're not religious—then don't sweat it. These two steps don't have to conjure up thoughts of 'cleansing of sin.' Basically, look at them this way: it's nice to do good to and for others. It's also nice to have others do the same for you. Chances are, most alcoholics have harmed or negatively impacted others at some point along the ride.

So let's make amends. Let others know what they mean to you and that you're changing. And also, try to stay away from people who have harmed *you*.

Step 10: "Continued to take personal inventory, and when we were wrong promptly admitted it."

Sure, admitting you've done 'wrong' isn't going to solve that problem. Still, this admission will at the least help to bring that problem to the forefront, instead of letting it sink into the booze abyss.

Admitting that we have a problem is about also admitting to other people. Thus, the group holds you accountable as well. If you come to realize that you did something wrong and for years you couldn't face it, it is always good to be honest about it. Better late than never, I say. Just like getting sober; better late than never.

Step 11: "Sought through prayer and meditation to improve our conscious contact with God as we understood God, praying only for knowledge of God's will for us and the power to carry that out."

Some argue that if AA were presented as a religious movement dedicated to comforting addicts, the program would not be so problematic. Unfortunately, say the critics, the program is disingenuous at best. Instead of being honest about what it is, it pretends to be appropriate for alcoholics of *all* religious and secular persuasions.

Again, this no longer bothers me. I think of "God" as good, orderly direction; and my "prayer and meditation"? Well… they are probably closer to 'self-talk' and 'open-mindedness'—but maybe I'm just splitting hairs.

The bottom line is: trust that the world can be a place of success for you. Get to know yourself and get to know what makes you feel alive. Be happy with being a sober, safe, and successful you.

Be happy with a new life and power.

Step 12: "Having had a spiritual awakening as the result of these steps, we tried to carry this message to other addicts and to practice these principles in all our affairs."

It's called Alcoholics "Anonymous" for a reason. Not everybody wants to advertise their inclusion in the group. Still, that doesn't mean they don't believe in the group. I've met plenty of members who speak of their addiction as a "spiritual malady" and if that's how they see it, so be it. Whatever works.

Many alcoholics will tell you that AA has opened their eyes to spirituality, and not necessarily religion. They will believe in a human connection and purpose, beyond just a randomness of existence. They feel that they can love people and love life without fear.

Some may call it spirituality, some may call it "God," some will call it the universality of spirit, the collective unconscious, the love of living and the acceptance of dying.

Call it what you will, and love it for what it is. If you want somebody to feel better about their addiction, to improve their circumstances, then let them know that the steps can help them. Don't force an individual to interpret the steps in any one way.

Their life, their way.

In the end, AA has helped keep me sober. I feel better about being sober, and I feel better about living my life in a way that I think is good.

I try not to think too hard when it comes to these steps, because for me, overthinking was what always got me into trouble. That's not to say I don't think deeply about other things, but when it comes to my addiction, ironically I think very little about it nowadays. And that seems to help.

Some people could tell you the exact day they got sober, but I can't. Frankly, I don't want to know. I can tell you years, but the exact day?

No way, Jose.

If you have tried AA, or know somebody who has tried AA, or think you or somebody you know should try AA, by all means… try AA!

If it 'fails,' there are plenty of other treatment options. You can read other books, and look up studies, and find clinics and therapies for this. It is best to use a combination of preventative and therapeutic measures. Support networks, groups, treatment plans, self-help, and even medication may all be required simultaneously.

Here are a few resources if you're interested in learning more:

Cognitive Behavioral Therapy—Overview

Drugs (Ask a doctor first)

General Alcoholism Info

Other Treatment Options

Alcohol Use Disorders

Negative Effects of Alcohol

About The Author

Thinking back, I should have died a hundred times.

The first time I got my hand on the sauce, I was young. Barely a teenager. It was a short glass of something old, the kind of special something my father kept stored away for cold winter nights spent in his blanket and armchair. I remember drinking it quickly, before anybody or *anything* found me guilty.

And then I remember sitting back, that sharp fire flowing through my throat and belly. It was a burn, and a warmth, and a sensation I would never forget.

Little did I know, this small innocuous drink would lead me through the hula-hoops of a lifespan of trouble. Little did I know that I was about to undergo a tumultuous ride to the other side—one that would bring me as close to the pearly white lights as anybody.

Even so, I was hard-pressed to call it "alcoholism."

Even as I found ways to procure my 'medicine,' nothing seemed terribly out of place. Sure, I kept the secret from my family, but that didn't make it a bad thing. For me, drinking wasn't some powerless craving. It was merely a liquid with a purpose.

What was wrong with that? Why couldn't I have a little fun?

As time went on, I kept my solo habits discreet. A slug there, a slug here—casual and necessary. Days took off with the sauce, you know, and there was no reason to see problems where there were none.

How could I *ever* see it as "dependency" or "addiction" or "abuse"? It was a part of my life and I was fine…

And I continued to feel fine.

I was merely a kid, trying to get by, trying to sift through the bogus and make my way. If being a little drunk helped me get there, then so be it. Besides, people could afford to take the edge off…

And it was the 70s, *dude*, so as far as I cared, alcohol was just the warm-up. The opening act. The prologue for a whole log of times to come.

Years went by, and I fell into patterns. Patterns brought problems, and problems landed me in programs; treatment programs where everybody *not* like me told me that I had a problem; that I was blind. That I was a full-blow "addict."

Problem was, I had no problem. And I knew this. I knew this every night when I stumbled home or swerved my car. Every morning when the bottle of Bourbon came out with the rising sun.

Despite these habits, I did what I wanted. I found myself an employer who knew nothing of my habits, and when the occasional tardiness crept upon me, I was always ready with a smile and an excuse.

Jobs didn't last long. I meandered, making my money here and there, finding shelter, finding booze, finding drugs, and miraculously finding a way to support myself, and my demons.

During the end of 1998, my life crumbled.

A person I had considered a rock for my whole life was no more. I saw them slip away; it was the first time I saw life literally drain from the human eyes. Those shiny cataracts giving way to a dull void.

When I left the hospital I was numb.

As I struggled to make sense of everything, I wondered about my own life. It struck me how fragile every moment really was; how quickly it could all go south.

Soon my job was gone. After years with the same employer, my tardiness had caught up. My work performance suffered, my attitude changed, my coworkers and bosses found that I was no longer the person they knew. Years of recommendations and promotions meant nothing. I was fired on the spot, and sent home without so much as a "goodbye."

Some mornings, I prayed that it would all just end.

And then the love of my life left me.

Our relationship had been in dire straits for a while, but I had turned my mind from that reality. When my partner finally left, I realized the truth. I was empty.

Without them, without the sources of meaning in my life, I began to fully spiral. I spent my days sleeping, drinking, milling about the dark, either hating everything or feeling nothing.

My friends were concerned about me. I wasn't returning their calls, I wasn't responding to texts or emails. I was sitting at home, collecting unemployment, and spending every last dollar I had at a liquor store up the street. Occasionally I'd catch myself squinting out the blinds of my small bedroom window, wondering if there was something, anything, out there for me.

My cycle continued.

Mornings began with vodka, evenings ended with rum. Every day the record replayed. Every day, I came to, the details of the previous day like smudges in a haze.

What was the point I'd ask? Why did any of it matter?

The bottle became my only solace. My only comfort. The thing that sustained me as it destroyed me.

The world continued to move forward, but I was sinking. What was the point in any of this mess? How could I possibly find value in a world that could end in the blink of an eye, a world where I was just another meaningless organism in the history of human existence?

How could I possibly do anything of importance? How could I ever *matter?*

It took me years, and drugs, and prison, and treatment, and enough hate and pain to ruin a man, to see what I had. And I believe it. If I could get clean—then so can you. Or somebody you know.

Remember, there is no telling how many chances we get in this thing called life. Addiction may be the hardest thing in the world to do, but it is *worth* fighting for. We are fighting our brains. We are fighting our genes. We are fighting our environment. We are fighting the very thing that constitutes our being.

But we are not alone. And believe me, there is an amazing world of opportunity out there if we want it… and if believe it and work for it, we can get it.

But that decision is yours. You can flop and flounder and never pull yourself up, or you can change today.

There is no reason why today can't be different. There is no reason why *you* can't be different.

So will you or won't you? The choice is yours. Will you put it off tomorrow, despite everything alcohol has done to your life, or will you make tomorrow today? Will you pick up another bottle, another beer, make another purchase, take another drink, take another risk, tell another lie, make another mistake?

Or will today be the day? What's it gonna be?

Who are *you* going to be?

***

A Special Note:

Thank you for reading "Last Call: Understanding and Treating the Alcoholic Brain." If you enjoyed this book and would like to read more like it, do not hesitate!

Join the mailing list TODAY and get instant updates about the freshest new content. As soon as a book is published on Amazon, you will be the first to know. Receive free, discounted, and new content the moment it becomes available!

Topics include: personal development, health improvement, psychological self-help, dietary solutions, fitness expertise, and much, *much* more!

Simply click below and enter your email address where prompted. It's that simple!

SUBSCRIBE

Other works by C.K. Murray:

1.   *Mindfulness Explained: The Mindful Solution to Stress, Depression, and Chronic Unhappiness*

www.ingramcontent.com/pod-product-compliance
Lightning Source LLC
Chambersburg PA
CBHW070138260726
48658CB00001B/477